Table Of Contents

Chapter 1: Introduction to Tax Benefits for Short-Term Rental Income

Understanding the Importance of Tax Planning for Homeowners

Owning a short-term rental property (STR) can be a lucrative side hustle or even a full-time income source. However, unlike traditional long-term rentals, STRs come with unique tax implications that require meticulous planning for optimal financial benefit, this book will go in detail about these in an easy to read and simple format.

Some of the advantages we will talk about include Maximizing Deductions. Short-term rentals offer a wider range of deductible expenses compared to traditional rentals. These include mortgage interest, property taxes, depreciation, utilities, repairs, maintenance, cleaning costs, advertising, and even home office expenses if you manage the rental remotely. Strategic record-keeping and understanding which expenses you can claim significantly reduce your taxable income. As well as Depreciation Boost. Depreciation allows you to deduct a portion of your property's value over its useful life from your taxes each year. Short-term rentals typically experience higher wear and tear than long-term rentals, potentially allowing you to claim a larger depreciation deduction and further lower your taxable income. We will go into more detail on these later on in the book.

Some of the tricky issues we will navigate are is it a business or hobby in the eyes of the IRS. he IRS differentiates between STRs operated as a business and those considered a hobby. Classifying your STR as a business unlocks access to more deductions and tax benefits. Consult a tax professional to ensure you meet the criteria and document your activities diligently. Another example of an issue we will discuss is SALT- State and Local Taxes as they pertain to short-term rentals.

Planning for the future is one of the key takeaways you should have from this book. Things like Capital Gains Tax are important to keep in mind and planned for accordingly. When you eventually sell your STR property, any profit you make is subject to capital gains tax. However, strategic planning like holding the property for the required minimum period or utilizing available exemptions can minimize your tax liability. Another is Retirement Planning. The income generated from your STR can significantly contribute to your retirement savings. By understanding the tax implications of reinvesting earnings or leveraging home equity loans, you can build a more secure financial future.

We will help you familiarize with Rental Income and Expense reporting with regards to how this is crucial for tax deductions. We will help you understand which amongst other things which expenses are deductible and to what extent, which tax form should you use Schedule E or Schedule C, the occupancy rule and its tax implications.

Overall, understanding the importance of tax planning is crucial for homeowners involved in rental properties. By familiarizing themselves with the various tax deductions, reporting requirements, and strategies, individuals can minimize their tax liability and maximize their overall tax benefits. Whether it's handling rental property losses, utilizing property management companies, or navigating IRS rules, this subchapter equips homeowners with the knowledge needed to strategize and optimize their tax benefits.

Overview of Airbnb and Vrbo as Short-Term Rental Platforms

Airbnb and Vrbo are two of the most prominent players in the short-term rental platform industry, each with a unique history and impact on the market.

Airbnb was founded in 2008 in San Francisco. It started as a simple idea by Brian Chesky and Joe Gebbia to rent out air mattresses in their living room to offset their rent. This concept quickly evolved into a global phenomenon. The platform allows homeowners and renters to list their spaces for short-term rentals, ranging from single rooms to entire houses. Airbnb revolutionized the way people travel, offering a more personalized and often more affordable alternative to traditional hotels. Over the years, it expanded its services to include experiences and adventures, further diversifying its offerings.

Vrbo, which stands for Vacation Rentals by Owner, was established earlier than Airbnb, in 1995. It was founded by David Clouse in Aurora, Colorado, as a way to list his ski resort property. Unlike Airbnb, Vrbo initially focused exclusively on vacation homes, targeting travelers looking for accommodations that offered home-like amenities and more space, often for extended stays. It became known for catering to families and larger groups. Over time, Vrbo also expanded and evolved, eventually being acquired by Expedia Group in 2015.

Both platforms have significantly influenced the travel industry. They've democratized access to travel accommodations, allowing anyone with a spare room or a second home to become a host. This has not only provided income opportunities for millions worldwide but also broadened the spectrum of accommodation options available to travelers. While they share similarities, Airbnb and Vrbo have distinct models and target markets, with Airbnb offering a wider range of accommodations and experiences, and Vrbo focusing more on larger properties and family-friendly rentals. Their growth and evolution continue to shape the landscape of short-term rentals, making them indispensable to the modern traveler.

Chapter 2: Tax Deductions

Maximizing Tax Deductions

For Airbnb and Vrbo hosts, adeptly navigating the realm of tax deductions is a crucial skill. This ability not only minimizes your tax obligations but also bolsters your overall profitability. This chapter delves into various strategies and insights to optimize your tax deductions as an STR host.

Foremost among tax strategies is diligent record-keeping. This means meticulously documenting every expense incurred – from cleaning and maintenance costs to the amenities offered to guests. Such thorough documentation enables you to claim these expenses as deductions, effectively reducing your taxable income.

A key aspect to consider is the tax implications of listing a room in your primary residence on Airbnb or Vrbo. Often, a portion of your mortgage interest, property taxes, and home insurance can be categorized as business expenditures, potentially qualifying for deductions. However, it's imperative to seek advice from a tax expert who can clarify the nuances and constraints applicable in your locale.

For those renting out vacation homes or secondary properties on Airbnb, there are unique deductions to explore, including property depreciation and expenses related to maintaining and managing these additional properties.

Additionally, hosts who list their properties across multiple platforms must meticulously track and accurately report all income to avoid legal repercussions and penalties. Utilizing professional accounting services or software is highly recommended to ensure precise and compliant tax filings.

Eco-conscious hosts have an added advantage. Many regions offer tax incentives for adopting sustainable practices like installing solar panels or using energy-efficient appliances. These green initiatives not only reduce your carbon footprint but also present an opportunity to maximize tax deductions.

Moreover, hosting events or parties at your short-term rental property brings its own set of tax considerations. The nature and scale of these events can influence the taxation process, necessitating a keen understanding of local regulations and potentially seeking guidance from a tax expert to ensure full compliance.

In summary, optimizing tax deductions as an STR host demands strategic planning, impeccable record-keeping, and a thorough understanding of local tax regulations. By adhering to the guidelines outlined in this chapter, you can effectively manage your tax liabilities, ensuring compliance and enhancing your profitability as an STR host.

Chapter 3: Tax Reporting and Filing

Filing Requirements

As an short-term rental host (STR) host, grasping the intricacies of tax compliance is fundamental to ensure you accurately report rental income and adhere to tax regulations. This subchapter aims to equip you with vital insights to proficiently navigate the tax landscape, allowing you to optimize your deductions while fulfilling your tax responsibilities.

Tax obligations for STR income can vary significantly based on your geographical location. It's imperative to acquaint yourself with the local rules and regulations. In some jurisdictions, this might involve acquiring a business license or registering as a short-term rental provider. Non-compliance can lead to penalties or legal challenges.

On the Federal level the tax requirements include:

1. Form 1040: Report STR income and expenses on Schedule E (for supplemental income) or Schedule C (if operating as a business).
2. Self-Employment Tax: If classified as a business, pay self-employment tax (Social Security and Medicare) on net earnings.
3. Estimated Taxes: Pay quarterly estimated taxes if you expect to owe $1,000 or more in taxes for the year.

The States, districts, cities also have their own taxes known as State and Local Tax with their own requirements:

1. Sales Tax: Collect and remit sales tax on rental charges in states with applicable laws.
2. Occupancy Taxes: Collect and pay local occupancy taxes (e.g., hotel or lodging taxes).
3. Business Licenses: Obtain necessary business licenses or permits required by your locality.

Then there are Specific Forms and Filings that are crucial to a successful filing and these are:

1. Form W-9: Provide this to rental platforms (like Airbnb or VRBO) to report your income to the IRS.
2. Form 1099-K: Receive this form from rental platforms if you meet certain payment thresholds.
3. Local Registration: Some cities or counties require registration of STRs, often with additional fees or taxes.

In summary, a thorough understanding of the tax filing requirements for STR hosts is essential for regulatory compliance and optimizing deductions. By maintaining precise records, staying informed about the tax rules in your area, and seeking professional advice as necessary, you can effectively manage the tax aspects of your STR hosting, ensuring both compliance and financial efficiency.

Schedule C or Schedule E?

As an STR host, deciphering the complexities of tax filing, particularly whether to use Schedule C or Schedule E, is an essential part of managing your rental income. This subchapter aims to clarify the distinctions between these schedules, assisting you in making an informed choice that aligns with your hosting activities.

Schedule C is tailored for hosts who engage in their rental activities more hands-on, akin to running a business. This includes offering comprehensive services to guests such as housekeeping, meals, or concierge assistance. If your hosting approach fits this description, Schedule C is likely more appropriate. It allows for a broader range of business-related deductions, encompassing advertising, maintenance, supplies, and property depreciation.

Conversely, Schedule E is more apt for hosts who adopt a passive role in their rental endeavors. If your involvement is limited to renting out part of your residence or an additional property without providing extensive guest services, Schedule E might be the better option. This schedule permits deductions for common rental expenses like mortgage interest, property taxes, insurance, cleaning costs, and property management fees.

The choice between Schedule C and Schedule E isn't universal; it hinges on individual factors such as your level of engagement in the rental process, the nature of services you provide, and the type of property rented. These elements collectively influence the most suitable tax schedule for your circumstances.

In summary, for STR hosts, selecting the appropriate tax schedule is a pivotal decision. Grasping the nuances of Schedule C and Schedule E, and possibly consulting a tax professional, will guide you to the optimal choice tailored to your specific rental situation. Informed decision-making in this regard not only facilitates tax savings but also ensures adherence to tax compliance standards.

An example of a Schedule C form:

SCHEDULE C
(Form 1040)

Department of the Treasury
Internal Revenue Service

Profit or Loss From Business
(Sole Proprietorship)

Go to *www.irs.gov/ScheduleC* for instructions and the latest information.

Attach to Form 1040, 1040-SR, 1040-NR, or 1041; partnerships must generally file Form 1065.

OMB No. 1545-0074

2022

Attachment
Sequence No. **09**

Name of proprietor | Social security number (SSN)

A Principal business or profession, including product or service (see instructions)

B Enter code from instructions

C Business name. If no separate business name, leave blank.

D Employer ID number (EIN) (see instr.)

E Business address (including suite or room no.) ....
City, town or post office, state, and ZIP code

F Accounting method: **(1)** ☐ Cash **(2)** ☐ Accrual **(3)** ☐ Other (specify) ....

G Did you "materially participate" in the operation of this business during 2022? If "No," see instructions for limit on losses . ☐ Yes ☐ No

H If you started or acquired this business during 2022, check here . . . . ☐

I Did you make any payments in 2022 that would require you to file Form(s) 1099? See instructions . . . . . ☐ Yes ☐ No

J If "Yes," did you or will you file required Form(s) 1099? . . . . ☐ Yes ☐ No

Part I Income

1	Gross receipts or sales. See instructions for line 1 and check the box if this income was reported to you on Form W-2 and the "Statutory employee" box on that form was checked . . . . ☐	**1**
2	Returns and allowances	**2**
3	Subtract line 2 from line 1	**3**
4	Cost of goods sold (from line 42)	**4**
5	**Gross profit.** Subtract line 4 from line 3	**5**
6	Other income, including federal and state gasoline or fuel tax credit or refund (see instructions) . . .	**6**
7	**Gross income.** Add lines 5 and 6	**7**

Part II Expenses. Enter expenses for business use of your home **only** on line 30.

8	Advertising	**8**	**18** Office expense (see instructions) .	**18**	
9	Car and truck expenses (see instructions) . . .	**9**	**19** Pension and profit-sharing plans .	**19**	
10	Commissions and fees .	**10**	**20** Rent or lease (see instructions):		
11	Contract labor (see instructions)	**11**	**a** Vehicles, machinery, and equipment	**20a**	
12	Depletion	**12**	**b** Other business property . .	**20b**	
13	Depreciation and section 179 expense deduction (not included in Part III) (see instructions)	**13**	**21** Repairs and maintenance . .	**21**	
			22 Supplies (not included in Part III) .	**22**	
			23 Taxes and licenses	**23**	
			24 Travel and meals:		
14	Employee benefit programs (other than on line 19) .	**14**	**a** Travel	**24a**	
15	Insurance (other than health)	**15**	**b** Deductible meals (see instructions)	**24b**	
16	Interest (see instructions):		**25** Utilities	**25**	
a	Mortgage (paid to banks, etc.)	**16a**	**26** Wages (less employment credits)	**26**	
b	Other	**16b**	**27a** Other expenses (from line 48) .	**27a**	
17	Legal and professional services	**17**	**b** **Reserved for future use** .	**27b**	
28	**Total expenses** before expenses for business use of home. Add lines 8 through 27a			**28**	
29	Tentative profit or (loss). Subtract line 28 from line 7			**29**	

30 Expenses for business use of your home. Do not report these expenses elsewhere. Attach Form 8829 unless using the simplified method. See instructions.
Simplified method filers only: Enter the total square footage of (a) your home: _____
and (b) the part of your home used for business: _____. Use the Simplified Method Worksheet in the instructions to figure the amount to enter on line 30 . . . . | **30** |

31 **Net profit or (loss).** Subtract line 30 from line 29.
• If a profit, enter on both **Schedule 1 (Form 1040), line 3,** and on **Schedule SE, line 2.** (If you checked the box on line 1, see instructions.) Estates and trusts, enter on **Form 1041, line 3.**
• If a loss, you **must** go to line 32. | **31** |

32 If you have a loss, check the box that describes your investment in this activity. See instructions.
• If you checked 32a, enter the loss on both **Schedule 1 (Form 1040), line 3,** and on **Schedule SE, line 2.** (If you checked the box on line 1, see the line 31 instructions.) Estates and trusts, enter on **Form 1041, line 3.**
• If you checked 32b, you **must** attach **Form 6198.** Your loss may be limited.

32a ☐ All investment is at risk.
32b ☐ Some investment is not at risk.

For Paperwork Reduction Act Notice, see the separate instructions. | Cat. No. 11334P | Schedule C (Form 1040) 2022

An Example of a Schedule E form:

SCHEDULE E
(Form 1040)

Department of the Treasury
Internal Revenue Service

Name(s) shown on return

Supplemental Income and Loss

(From rental real estate, royalties, partnerships, S corporations, estates, trusts, REMICs, etc.)

Attach to Form 1040, 1040-SR, 1040-NR, or 1041.
Go to *www.irs.gov/ScheduleE* for instructions and the latest information.

OMB No. 1545-0074

2023

Attachment
Sequence No. **13**

Your social security number

Part I   **Income or Loss From Rental Real Estate and Royalties**

Note: If you are in the business of renting personal property, use **Schedule C**. See instructions. If you are an individual, report farm rental income or loss from **Form 4835** on page 2, line 40.

A   Did you make any payments in 2023 that would require you to file Form(s) 1099? See instructions . . . . . ☐ Yes ☐ No
B   If "Yes," did you or will you file required Form(s) 1099? . . . . ☐ Yes ☐ No

1a   Physical address of each property (street, city, state, ZIP code)

A	
B	
C	

1b	Type of Property (from list below)	2	For each rental real estate property listed above, report the number of fair rental and personal use days. Check the QJV box only if you meet the requirements to file as a qualified joint venture. See instructions.		Fair Rental Days	Personal Use Days	QJV
A				A			☐
B				B			☐
C				C			☐

Type of Property:

1 Single Family Residence   3 Vacation/Short-Term Rental   5 Land   7 Self-Rental
2 Multi-Family Residence   4 Commercial   6 Royalties   8 Other (describe) _____

			Properties:		
			A	B	C
Income:					
3	Rents received	3			
4	Royalties received	4			
Expenses:					
5	Advertising	5			
6	Auto and travel (see instructions)	6			
7	Cleaning and maintenance	7			
8	Commissions	8			
9	Insurance	9			
10	Legal and other professional fees	10			
11	Management fees	11			
12	Mortgage interest paid to banks, etc. (see instructions)	12			
13	Other interest	13			
14	Repairs	14			
15	Supplies	15			
16	Taxes	16			
17	Utilities	17			
18	Depreciation expense or depletion	18			
19	Other (list) _____	19			
20	Total expenses. Add lines 5 through 19	20			
21	Subtract line 20 from line 3 (rents) and/or 4 (royalties). If result is a (loss), see instructions to find out if you must file **Form 6198**	21			
22	Deductible rental real estate loss after limitation, if any, on **Form 8582** (see instructions)	22	( )	( )	( )

23a	Total of all amounts reported on line 3 for all rental properties	23a		
b	Total of all amounts reported on line 4 for all royalty properties	23b		
c	Total of all amounts reported on line 12 for all properties	23c		
d	Total of all amounts reported on line 18 for all properties	23d		
e	Total of all amounts reported on line 20 for all properties	23e		
24	**Income.** Add positive amounts shown on line 21. Do not include any losses	24	
25	**Losses.** Add royalty losses from line 21 and rental real estate losses from line 22. Enter total losses here	25	( )
26	**Total rental real estate and royalty income or (loss).** Combine lines 24 and 25. Enter the result here. If Parts II, III, and IV, and line 40 on page 2 do not apply to you, also enter this amount on Schedule 1 (Form 1040), line 5. Otherwise, include this amount in the total on line 41 on page 2 .	26	

For Paperwork Reduction Act Notice, see the separate instructions.   Cat. No. 11344L   Schedule E (Form 1040) 2023

Understanding the Reporting Requirements for Rental Income

Understanding the reporting requirements for rental income from short-term rentals (STRs) is crucial for property owners to ensure compliance with tax laws and avoid potential penalties. Here are some key aspects of reporting rental income from STRs. All income received from short-term rentals must be reported on your tax return. This includes payments for nightly or weekly rentals, as well as any additional fees charged to renters (like cleaning fees or pet fees).Typically, this income is reported on Schedule E (Form 1040), "Supplemental Income and Loss" unless after reading the subchapter above you decided to use Schedule C. Always consult your tax professional if you are not sure on which forms to use.

There is also an occupancy rule you need to be familiar with. If you rent your property for fewer than 15 days during the year, you don't have to report the rental income. However, you also can't deduct any expenses as rental expenses. If rented out for more than 14 days, all rental income must be reported, but you're also allowed to deduct related expenses.

As a homeowner or renter who earns income from short-term rentals through platforms like Airbnb and Vrbo, it is important to understand the reporting requirements for rental income. Failing to comply with these requirements can result in penalties or even an audit by the IRS.

To accurately report your rental income, it is advisable to keep detailed records of all transactions. This includes documenting the dates of rental periods, rental amounts, and any expenses incurred in relation to the rental property. By maintaining comprehensive records, you can ensure that you report your rental income accurately and take advantage of the tax deductions available to you.

In conclusion, understanding the reporting requirements for rental income is essential for homeowners who earn income from short-term rentals. By accurately reporting rental income, maximizing deductions, and complying with IRS rules, you can strategize your tax benefits effectively and make the most of your rental property ventures.

Forms and Schedules for Reporting Airbnb and Vrbo Income

When it comes to reporting your Airbnb and Vrbo rental income on your tax returns, there are specific forms and schedules that homeowners need to be aware of. Understanding the appropriate paperwork is crucial to ensure compliance with IRS regulations and maximize your tax benefits. In this subchapter, we will discuss the various forms and schedules you need to be familiar with when reporting your short-term rental income.

The primary form that you will need to file is the Schedule E, Supplemental Income and Loss. This form is used to report rental income and expenses from your Airbnb and Vrbo properties. On Schedule E, you will report your rental income, deductible expenses, and calculate your net rental income or loss.

Additionally, if you have a property management company handling your rentals, you may also need to file Form 1099-MISC, Miscellaneous Income, to report the fees paid to the management company. This form is necessary if you pay the property management company more than $600 in a tax year.

Another important form to be aware of is Form 4562, Depreciation and Amortization. This form is used to report the depreciation of your rental property and any improvements made during the year. Depreciation is a valuable tax deduction that allows you to recover the cost of your property over time.

It's essential to understand the IRS rules on rental property depreciation recapture. If you sell your rental property at a gain, the IRS may require you to recapture a portion of the depreciation you claimed and pay taxes on it. Form 4797, Sales of Business Property, is used to report the sale of your rental property and calculate any depreciation recapture.

In addition to these forms, it's important to keep detailed records of your rental income and expenses. This includes receipts for maintenance and repairs, as these expenses can be deductible. Understanding deductible expenses for maintenance and repairs is crucial to ensure you are maximizing your tax benefits.

In conclusion, reporting Airbnb and Vrbo rental income requires homeowners to be familiar with various forms and schedules. The Schedule E, Form 1099-MISC, Form 4562, and Form 4797 are some of the essential forms that need to be filed. Understanding the IRS rules on rental property depreciation, deductible expenses, and depreciation recapture is crucial to strategize tax benefits effectively. By staying organized and knowledgeable about the necessary paperwork, you can ensure compliance with IRS regulations and make the most of your short-term rental income.

Recordkeeping and Documentation for Rental Income Reporting

One of the key aspects of managing rental properties, whether residential or commercial, is keeping accurate records and maintaining proper documentation for rental income reporting. This subchapter aims to provide homeowners with valuable insights into the importance of recordkeeping and the necessary documentation required for reporting rental income.

For rental income, keep a detailed record of all rental income received, including dates and amounts for each booking. If you have any additional charges make sure that you document any extra fees charged, such as cleaning fees, pet fees, or late check-out fees. It is always good to also retain copies of booking confirmations from rental platforms or direct bookings, incase the IRS asks for them.

For expenses, keep receipts for all maintenance and repair expenses related to the rental property. Save utility bills if utilities are included in the rental cost or if the property is solely used for rental purposes. Document expenses for cleaning supplies, welcome gifts for guests, and service fees from rental platforms or property managers. If you use a Property Management company keep records of the fees paid.

Preserve closing statements or other documents that show the purchase price and expenses related to acquiring the property as well as any improvements or significant repairs. This is necessary because these can affect depreciation calculations and you will need to substantiate where the numbers came from if asked by the IRS.

When your mortgage company sends you the 1098 Mortgage Interest Statement keep it along with records of insurance premiums paid for coverage on the rental property. Also keep documentation of property tax payments if not on your form 1098. If your locality charges local occupancy or tourism taxes, these will not show up on your Form 1098. As a result you will need to maintain records of these payments.

Guest communication and agreements need to be retained as well. If you use rental agreements or terms and conditions for guests, keep copies of these documents. In addition retain records of significant communications with guests, especially if they relate to agreements or disputes.

Another important thing that STR hosts need is to maintain a calendar of rental activity, documenting when the property was rented and when it was used for personal purposes. Keep a log of maintenance and servicing activities to track expenses and property upkeep.

Generally, tax records should be kept for at least three years after filing the tax return. Some records related to property acquisition and improvements should be kept longer. In this digital age consider using digital tools or property management software for tracking income and expenses, which can simplify recordkeeping and reporting.

whenever you are in doubt or not sure about anything consider consulting with a tax professional or accountant who has expertise in STR taxation. They can provide guidance on recordkeeping and deductions.

Conclusion

Effective recordkeeping for STRs involves systematically documenting all aspects of rental activity, including income, expenses, improvements, and guest interactions. This not only helps in accurate tax reporting but also aids in understanding the financial performance of your rental business. Regularly updating and organizing these records ensures preparedness for tax time and any potential audits.

When it comes to tax deductions for residential and commercial rental properties, it is crucial to have detailed records of all expenses related to the property. This includes invoices, receipts, and other relevant documents that substantiate the expenses claimed. By maintaining organized records, homeowners can ensure they are maximizing their tax deductions and minimizing their tax liability.

For those using platforms like Airbnb and Vrbo to generate rental income, reporting this income on tax returns is essential. Homeowners need to understand the specific reporting requirements set forth by the Internal Revenue Service (IRS). This subchapter will provide clear guidelines on how to accurately report rental income from these platforms and avoid potential tax penalties.

Chapter 4: Tax Implications of Renting out space in Your Primary Residence

Allocating Expenses and Deductions for Mixed-Use Properties

One of the key considerations for STR hosts is how to properly allocate expenses and deductions for mixed-use properties. If you rent out living space to other people, it is important to understand the tax implications and strategies to maximize deductions while staying compliant with the tax laws.

Tax Tips for STR Hosts

As an STR host, there are several tax tips that can help you save money and reduce your tax burden. One important tip is to keep detailed records of all your expenses related to your rental property. This includes receipts for repairs, maintenance, cleaning services, and any other expenses directly related to hosting guests. By keeping accurate records, you can ensure that you claim all eligible deductions on your tax return.

Tax Deductions for STR Hosts

There are various tax deductions available for STR hosts. These deductions can help offset the income earned from renting out your property. Some of the common deductions include mortgage interest, property taxes, insurance premiums, utilities, and depreciation.

However, it is important to note that deductions may vary depending on the percentage of your property that is used for rental purposes.

Tax Reporting and Filing for STR Income

Reporting and filing your STR income is a crucial step to remain compliant with tax laws. In many countries or states, STR hosts are required to report their rental income on their tax returns. It is essential to accurately report your income and expenses to avoid penalties or audits. Additionally, you may be required to collect and remit sales taxes or occupancy taxes, depending on your jurisdiction.

Tax Implications of Renting out a Room in Your Primary Residence

If you are renting out a room in your primary residence on STR, there are specific tax considerations to keep in mind. In some cases, you may be eligible for the home office deduction, which allows you to deduct a portion of your home expenses based on the square footage used for rental purposes. However, it is important to consult with a tax professional to ensure that you meet all the requirements for claiming this deduction.

Tax Strategies for Maximizing Deductions as an STR Host

To maximize deductions as an STR host, it is important to keep accurate records, separate personal and rental expenses, and consult with a tax professional. By properly allocating expenses and taking advantage of eligible deductions, you can minimize your tax liability and maximize your savings.

Tax Benefits and Incentives for Eco-Friendly STR Hosts

If you are an eco-friendly host, there may be tax benefits and incentives available to you. Some jurisdictions offer tax credits or deductions for energy-efficient upgrades to your rental property, such as solar panels or energy-efficient appliances. These incentives can not only help you save money but also contribute to a sustainable future.

Tax Planning for Hosts who also Rent out their Property on Other Platforms

If you rent out your property on multiple platforms, such as STR and other vacation rental websites, it is important to have a tax planning strategy in place. This includes keeping separate records for each platform and understanding the tax implications and reporting requirements for each source of rental income.

Tax Implications of Renting out a Vacation Home or Second Property

If you own a vacation home or a second property that you rent out on STR, there are specific tax considerations to be aware of. In some cases, you may be subject to additional taxes, such as the vacation rental tax or transient occupancy tax. It is essential to understand the local regulations and consult with a tax professional to ensure compliance.

Tax Tips for Hosts Hosting Events or Parties on their Property

If you host events or parties on your property as an STR host, there are additional tax implications to consider. Depending on the size and type of event, you may be required to collect and remit sales taxes or obtain a special events permit. It is important to understand the local regulations and consult with a tax professional to ensure compliance.

Tax Implications of Renting out a Portion of Your Property or a Shared Space

If you rent out a portion of your property or a shared space on STR or Vrbo, you may have unique tax implications. In some cases, you may be eligible for the home-sharing exemption, which allows you to exclude a portion of your rental income from taxation. However, it is important to understand the specific requirements and consult with a tax professional to ensure compliance.

In conclusion, as a person who rents out living space to others, understanding the tax implications and strategies for allocating expenses and deductions for mixed-use properties is crucial. By following the tax tips for STR hosts, maximizing deductions, and staying compliant with tax reporting and filing requirements, you can save money and ensure a smooth and successful hosting experience. Remember to consult with a tax professional to tailor your tax strategies to your specific situation and jurisdiction.

Home Office Deduction for Rental Activities

One of the most valuable tax deductions available to STR hosts who rent out living space is the home office deduction. If you use a separate area in your home exclusively for your rental activities, you may be eligible to claim this deduction and potentially save a significant amount of money on your taxes.

To qualify for the home office deduction, you must meet certain requirements. First, the space you use for your rental activities must be used regularly and exclusively for that purpose. This means that it should be a dedicated area solely for your STR business, such as a spare bedroom or an office space.

Second, the home office must be your principal place of business. If you conduct the majority of your rental activities from this space, such as managing bookings, communicating with guests, and handling paperwork, then it likely meets this requirement.

To calculate the home office deduction, you have two options: the simplified method or the regular method. The simplified method allows you to deduct $5 per square foot of the area used for your rental activities, up to a maximum of 300 square feet. This method is simpler and requires less record-keeping.

Alternatively, you can use the regular method, which requires you to determine the actual expenses associated with your home office. This includes expenses such as rent, mortgage interest, utilities, insurance, and maintenance. The percentage of these expenses that can be deducted is based on the percentage of your home that is used for your rental activities.

It's important to keep detailed records of your expenses to support your home office deduction. This includes keeping track of receipts, invoices, and other relevant documents. You should also take photos or create a floor plan to show the specific area used for your rental activities.

Remember that the home office deduction is subject to certain limitations and restrictions, so it's recommended to consult with a tax professional or use tax software to ensure you are taking full advantage of this deduction while staying compliant with tax laws.

In conclusion, the home office deduction is a valuable tax benefit that can help STR hosts who rent out living space to save money on their taxes. By meeting the requirements and keeping accurate records, you can maximize your deductions and potentially reduce your tax liability.

Reporting Rental Income from a Room Rental on Airbnb or Vrbo

Renting out living space on platforms like Airbnb has become a popular way for people to earn extra income. However, it's important for hosts to understand the tax implications and reporting requirements associated with this type of rental income. This subchapter will provide valuable tax tips for Airbnb hosts who rent out a room in their primary residence.

Reporting rental income from a room rental on Airbnb or Vrbo is an essential step in staying compliant with tax regulations. The Internal Revenue Service (IRS) requires hosts to report all rental income, including income from short-term rentals. Failure to report this income can result in penalties and fines.

To accurately report rental income, hosts should keep detailed records of all rental transactions. This includes documenting the dates of each rental period, the amount received from each guest, and any expenses incurred. These records will be crucial when it comes time to file taxes.

When reporting rental income, hosts can take advantage of various tax deductions to minimize their tax liability. Deductions may include expenses such as advertising fees, cleaning costs, repairs, and maintenance. It's important to keep receipts and invoices for these expenses to support any deductions claimed.

For hosts who also rent out their property on other platforms, tax planning becomes even more critical. Different platforms may have different reporting requirements, and hosts must understand how to accurately report income from each platform.

Additionally, hosts who rent out a vacation home or second property on Airbnb may face different tax implications. It's important to understand the rules surrounding these types of rentals, as they can vary from renting out a room in your primary residence.

Lastly, hosts who host events or parties on their property should be aware of any specific tax tips and implications associated with these types of rentals. Depending on the nature of the event, additional tax considerations may apply.

In conclusion, reporting rental income from a room rental on Airbnb is crucial for hosts to stay compliant with tax regulations. By keeping detailed records, understanding tax deductions, and consulting with a tax professional, hosts can maximize deductions, minimize tax liability, and ensure compliance with local tax laws.

Chapter 5: Deductible Expenses for Maintenance and Repairs for Rental Properties

Differentiating Between Maintenance and Repairs for Tax Purposes

As an STR host, it is crucial to understand the difference between maintenance and repairs for tax purposes. While both expenses are necessary for keeping your rental property in top shape, they are treated differently when it comes to tax deductions. By understanding these distinctions, you can maximize your deductions and avoid any potential tax pitfalls.

Maintenance refers to the routine tasks and expenses required to keep your rental property in good condition. This includes regular cleaning, lawn care, pest control, and other similar activities. These expenses are considered part of the cost of doing business and are fully deductible. It is important to keep detailed records of these expenses, including receipts and invoices, to substantiate your deductions.

On the other hand, repairs are expenses incurred to fix or replace something that is broken or damaged. This could include fixing a leaky roof, replacing a broken window, or repairing appliances. Unlike maintenance expenses, repairs are treated differently for tax purposes. Instead of being fully deductible in the year they are incurred, repairs are generally capitalized and depreciated over time.

The IRS has specific rules regarding repairs that you must follow to ensure compliance. If a repair is considered a capital improvement, meaning it adds value to the property or extends its useful life, it should be capitalized and depreciated. However, if the repair is considered a restoration or replacement of a major component of the property, it may be considered a deductible expense.

To determine whether an expense is a repair or a capital improvement, you should consider the nature, purpose, and scope of the work performed. It is advisable to consult with a tax professional who can guide you through the specific rules and regulations applicable to your situation.

Understanding the difference between maintenance and repairs is crucial for accurate tax reporting and maximum deductions. By properly categorizing your expenses, you can ensure that you take advantage of all available deductions while staying compliant with tax laws. Remember to keep detailed records and consult with a tax professional to ensure you are making the most of your tax benefits as an STR host.

In conclusion, as an STR host, it is important to differentiate between maintenance and repairs for tax purposes. While maintenance expenses are fully deductible, repairs may need to be capitalized and depreciated over time. By understanding the rules and regulations surrounding these expenses, you can navigate the tax landscape more effectively and maximize your deductions.

Identifying Deductible Expenses for Routine Maintenance

As an STR host, it is important to understand which expenses are deductible for routine maintenance in order to maximize your tax savings. By identifying these deductible expenses, you can reduce your taxable income and potentially receive a larger refund. In this subchapter, we will discuss the various deductible expenses that you should be aware of as a host who rents out living space to other people.

One of the key deductions for STR hosts is the cost of routine maintenance and repairs. This includes expenses such as cleaning supplies, replacement of linens and towels, and general upkeep of your property. These expenses are considered ordinary and necessary for the operation of your STR business, making them eligible for deduction.

Additionally, any fees paid to professional cleaners or maintenance personnel can also be deducted. If you hire a cleaning service to sanitize your property before and after each guest's stay, or if you rely on professionals to handle repairs and maintenance tasks, you can deduct these expenses as well.

It's important to note that only expenses directly related to your STR business are deductible. If you use a portion of your property for personal use, such as a bedroom or shared space, you can only deduct the expenses that are associated with the rental portion. This means that you will need to calculate the percentage of these expenses that is directly attributable to your STR business.

Furthermore, expenses for repairs and maintenance that are considered capital improvements, such as renovations or major upgrades, cannot be deducted in the year they are incurred. Instead, these expenses must be depreciated over a period of time. It is recommended to consult with a tax professional to determine the appropriate depreciation schedule for these expenses.

In conclusion, understanding which expenses are deductible for routine maintenance is crucial for STR hosts. By keeping track of these expenses and properly documenting them, you can reduce your taxable income and maximize your tax savings. Remember to consult with a tax professional for personalized advice based on your specific circumstances.

Understanding Capital Improvements and their tax treatment

As an STR host, it's essential to understand the concept of capital improvements and how they are treated for tax purposes. Capital improvements are significant renovations or additions made to your property that enhance its value, prolong its useful life, or adapt it to a new use. These improvements go beyond routine repairs and maintenance and typically involve substantial investments of time and money.

The tax treatment of capital improvements is different from that of ordinary repairs and maintenance. While repairs and maintenance expenses are deductible in the year they are incurred, capital improvements are not fully deductible in the year they are made. Instead, they are added to the basis of your property and are depreciated over time.

Adding capital improvements to your property's basis can be beneficial as it reduces your taxable gain when you eventually sell the property. The basis is the original cost of the property plus the cost of any capital improvements made, minus any depreciation claimed. By increasing the basis, you effectively decrease the taxable gain, resulting in potential tax savings.

It's important to note that not all expenses related to your property qualify as capital improvements. Regular repairs and maintenance, such as fixing a leaky faucet or repainting a room, are considered deductible expenses. However, if you replace the entire plumbing system or renovate the entire room, these would be considered capital improvements.

To determine if an expense is a capital improvement, consider the following factors:

1. Significance: Is the expense substantial and significantly enhances the property's value or extends its useful life?

2. Adaptation: Does the expense adapt the property to a new use or improve it beyond its original condition?

3. Improvement: Does the expense improve the property's functionality, efficiency, or aesthetics?

When it comes to tax reporting and filing, it is crucial to keep accurate records of all capital improvements made to your property. This includes invoices, receipts, and any relevant documentation. Additionally, consult with a tax professional or CPA to ensure you are correctly accounting for these expenses and maximizing your deductions.

Understanding the tax treatment of capital improvements is especially important for STR hosts who rent out their primary residence or vacation home. These hosts may be eligible for various tax deductions, benefits, and incentives, but it's essential to navigate the complex tax rules and regulations specific to your country or state.

Capital improvements can provide long-term benefits and potential tax savings for STR hosts. By understanding the tax treatment of these improvements and keeping accurate records, hosts can maximize their deductions and stay compliant with tax laws. Consult with a tax professional to ensure you are taking full advantage of the tax benefits available to you as an STR host.

Advertising and Marketing costs

As an STR host, it's essential to understand the various tax implications and deductions related to your rental income. One area that often confuses many hosts is advertising and marketing costs. In this subchapter, we will explore the tax tips and considerations regarding these expenses.

When it comes to advertising and marketing your STR property, you can deduct the costs associated with promoting and attracting guests. This includes expenses such as creating and maintaining a website, online listings, professional photography, and even printing brochures or business cards. These costs are considered ordinary and necessary for your rental business, making them eligible for tax deductions.

It's important to keep detailed records of your advertising and marketing expenses. This includes invoices, receipts, and any other documentation that proves the legitimacy of the costs. By maintaining accurate records, you ensure that you can claim these deductions when filing your taxes.

Additionally, if you hire a marketing agency or a professional photographer to promote your STR property, their fees are also deductible. Be sure to obtain proper documentation and receipts for these services as well.

In some cases, as an STR host, you may choose to host events or parties on your property. If you incur advertising and marketing expenses specific to these events, such as promoting the party or hiring a DJ, these costs can also be deducted. However, it's crucial to distinguish between personal and business expenses. Only the portion directly related to your rental business is eligible for deductions.

It's worth noting that tax regulations and deductions for STR hosts can vary depending on the country or state you reside in. Therefore, it's crucial to consult a tax professional who specializes in STR taxation or thoroughly research the specific tax laws in your location.

In summary, as an STR host, advertising and marketing costs are tax-deductible expenses that can help you reduce your taxable income. By keeping accurate records and understanding the specific rules and regulations related to your location, you can maximize your deductions and ensure compliance with tax laws. Remember to consult with a tax professional or conduct thorough research to fully understand the tax implications of your STR rental business.

Keeping Accurate Records for Tax Purposes

As an STR host, it is essential to keep accurate records for tax purposes. Maintaining detailed records will not only save you time and stress during tax season but also help you maximize tax deductions and stay compliant with tax laws. In this subchapter, we will explore the importance of record-keeping for STR hosts and provide useful tips to help you maintain accurate records.

One of the key reasons to keep accurate records is to ensure that you report your STR income correctly. Failure to report your income accurately can result in penalties or audits by tax authorities. By maintaining organized records, you can easily track your rental income, including the dates and amounts received from each booking. This will make it easier to report your STR income when filing your taxes.

Additionally, keeping detailed records will enable you to claim all eligible tax deductions. As an STR host, you are entitled to several deductions, such as cleaning fees, maintenance costs, and supplies. However, to claim these deductions, you must have proper documentation to support your expenses. By keeping receipts, invoices, and other relevant documents, you can ensure that you have the necessary evidence to claim deductions and reduce your taxable income.

Furthermore, accurate record-keeping will be beneficial if you ever face an audit. In the event of an audit, you will need to provide evidence to support your reported income and deductions. By having well-organized records, you can easily provide the required documentation and demonstrate your compliance with tax laws.

To maintain accurate records, consider utilizing digital tools and software. Many accounting software and mobile apps are specifically designed for STR hosts to track income, expenses, and other financial records. These tools can automate record-keeping processes, making it easier for you to stay organized and maintain accurate records.

In conclusion, keeping accurate records is crucial for STR hosts. By maintaining detailed and organized records, you can accurately report your STR income, claim eligible tax deductions, and stay compliant with tax laws. Utilizing digital tools can simplify the record-keeping process and help you maximize your tax benefits. Remember, accurate record-keeping not only saves you time and stress but also ensures that you are taking full advantage of the tax benefits available to you as an STR host.

Working with a Tax Professional for Optimal Deductions

As an STR host, understanding the tax implications of renting out your living space is crucial to staying compliant and maximizing your deductions. While there are numerous resources available to help you navigate the complex world of taxes, working with a tax professional can provide you with expert guidance tailored to your specific situation.

One of the key benefits of partnering with a tax professional is their in-depth knowledge of tax deductions for STR hosts. They can help you identify all the eligible expenses that can be claimed as deductions, such as cleaning fees, repairs and maintenance, insurance, utilities, and even the cost of furnishing your rental property. By ensuring that you are taking advantage of every available deduction, you can significantly reduce your taxable income and save money in the process.

Tax reporting and filing for STR income can be overwhelming, especially if you are not well-versed in tax laws. A tax professional can assist you in correctly reporting your STR income, ensuring that you comply with all necessary tax regulations. They can also guide you through the process of filing your tax return, making sure that you meet all filing deadlines and avoid potential penalties or audits.

If you are renting out a room in your primary residence on Airbnb, the tax implications can be different compared to renting out an entire property. A tax professional can help you understand the specific rules and regulations that apply to your situation, such as the home office deduction and the allocation of expenses between personal and rental use.

For Airbnb hosts operating in different countries or states, navigating the tax considerations can be even more complex. A tax professional who specializes in international or state-specific tax laws can help you understand your obligations and take advantage of any unique tax benefits or incentives available in your location.

Additionally, if you rent out your property on multiple platforms or also use it for personal use, a tax professional can assist you in developing tax strategies to optimize your deductions. They can help you determine the proportion of expenses that can be claimed as deductions and provide guidance on record-keeping requirements.

Furthermore, if you are an eco-friendly STR host, there may be special tax benefits and incentives available to you. A tax professional can help you identify and take advantage of these opportunities, potentially saving you even more money while promoting sustainable practices.

Lastly, if you host events or parties on your property or rent out a portion of your property or a shared space, the tax implications may vary. Working with a tax professional can help you understand the specific rules that apply to these situations and ensure that you meet all tax obligations.

In conclusion, partnering with a tax professional can be highly beneficial for STR hosts. They can provide expert guidance on tax deductions, assist with tax reporting and filing, navigate specific tax considerations, and help you develop tax strategies for optimal deductions. By working with a tax professional, you can stay compliant, save money, and focus on providing an exceptional experience for your STR guests.

Chapter 6: IRS Rules on Depreciation for Rental Properties

Depreciation Basics: What You Need to Know

Depreciation is a fundamental concept that every STR host should understand when it comes to tax planning and maximizing deductions. In this subchapter, we will delve into the basics of depreciation and how it can benefit you as a host.

Depreciation is essentially the wear and tear that occurs to your property over time. As an STR host, you can take advantage of this concept to claim deductions for the decline in value of certain assets used in your rental business.

One important thing to note is that depreciation can only be claimed for assets that have a limited useful life, such as furniture, appliances, and even the property itself. Land, on the other hand, is not eligible for depreciation deductions, as it is considered to have an indefinite useful life.

To calculate depreciation, you will need to determine the cost basis of the asset, the estimated useful life, and the depreciation method. The most common method used by STR hosts is the Modified Accelerated Cost Recovery System (MACRS).

By depreciating your assets, you can spread out the deduction over several years, rather than taking the entire cost as a deduction in one year. This can help to reduce your taxable income and lower your overall tax liability.

It's important to note that there are certain rules and limitations when it comes to depreciation. For example, the property must be used for business purposes at least part of the time in order to claim depreciation. Additionally, there are specific rules for claiming depreciation on your primary residence if you rent out a portion of it on STR.

Furthermore, different countries or states may have their own rules and regulations regarding depreciation. It's crucial to stay informed about the tax considerations and implications relevant to your specific location.

In conclusion, depreciation is a powerful tool for STR hosts to reduce their tax liability and maximize deductions. By understanding the basics of depreciation and staying up-to-date with the relevant rules and regulations, you can take full advantage of this tax strategy to save money and stay compliant as an STR host.

Determining the Depreciable Basis of a Rental Property

As an STR host or someone who rents out living space to others, it's crucial to understand the concept of the depreciable basis of your rental property. The depreciable basis is the value of your property that can be depreciated over time, resulting in tax deductions that can save you money. In this subchapter, we will explore how to determine the depreciable basis of your rental property and maximize your tax benefits.

The depreciable basis is calculated based on the original cost of the property, including the purchase price, closing costs, and any improvements made. It's important to note that land is not depreciable, so the basis should only include the value of the building and its improvements. To determine the depreciable basis accurately, you may need to consult with a tax professional or refer to IRS guidelines relevant to your country or state.

For hosts who rent out a room in their primary residence on Airbnb, determining the depreciable basis can be a bit more complicated. In these cases, only the portion of the property used for rental purposes can be considered for depreciation. This means you will need to calculate the percentage of your home used exclusively for rental activities and apply that percentage to the original cost and improvements.

If you rent out a vacation home or a second property on Airbnb, the depreciable basis is typically determined using the same principles as a regular rental property. However, be aware that special rules may apply if you use the property for personal use for a certain number of days each year. Again, consulting a tax professional is recommended to ensure compliance with tax regulations.

Maximizing your tax deductions as an STR host requires careful record-keeping. Keep track of all expenses related to the rental property, including repairs, maintenance, mortgage interest, property taxes, and insurance. These costs can be deducted from your rental income, reducing your taxable income.

Understanding and determining the depreciable basis of your rental property is essential for STR hosts and individuals renting out living spaces. It allows you to take advantage of tax deductions and maximize your tax benefits. Ensure you accurately calculate the depreciable basis by considering the original cost, improvements made, and any specific rules or regulations applicable to your situation. By doing so, you can save money and stay compliant with tax laws as an STR host.

Depreciation Methods and Recovery Periods

When it comes to being an STR host, it's important to understand the various tax implications and deductions available to you. One key aspect of tax planning is understanding depreciation methods and recovery periods for the property you are renting out. This subchapter will provide you with essential information on how to maximize your tax benefits and stay compliant.

Depreciation is the gradual loss of value over time for property used in a business or income-producing activity. As an STR host, you can depreciate the portion of your property that is used for rental purposes. This includes the house itself, as well as any furniture, appliances, or other assets used to furnish the rental space.

There are different depreciation methods available, such as the straight-line method and the accelerated depreciation method. The straight-line method allows you to deduct an equal amount each year over the recovery period determined by the IRS. On the other hand, the accelerated depreciation method allows for larger deductions in the earlier years of the recovery period, resulting in higher tax savings upfront.

The recovery period is the number of years over which you can depreciate your property. For residential rental properties, the recovery period is typically 27.5 years. However, some assets may have a shorter recovery period, such as furniture or appliances, which can be depreciated over 5 or 7 years.

It's important to note that the recovery period starts when the property is placed in service for rental purposes. This means that if you started renting out a room on Airbnb in the middle of the year, you can still claim depreciation for that portion of the year.

To maximize your deductions, it's crucial to keep accurate records of the purchase price and improvement costs of your property. This includes documenting any upgrades or renovations made to the rental space. By doing so, you can determine the basis for depreciation and ensure you are claiming the appropriate deductions.

In addition, it's essential to stay informed about any changes in tax laws and regulations that may affect your depreciation deductions. Tax laws can vary between countries or states, so it's important to consult with a tax professional who specializes in STR tax reporting and filing.

Understanding depreciation methods and recovery periods can significantly impact your tax savings as an STR host. By utilizing the appropriate depreciation method and recovery period, you can maximize deductions and stay compliant with tax regulations. Remember to keep accurate records and consult with a tax professional to ensure you are taking advantage of all available tax benefits.

Form 4562

Form 4562

Department of the Treasury
Internal Revenue Service

Depreciation and Amortization
(Including Information on Listed Property)
Attach to your tax return.
Go to *www.irs.gov/Form4562* for instructions and the latest information.

OMB No. 1545-0172

2023

Attachment
Sequence No. **179**

Name(s) shown on return	Business or activity to which this form relates	Identifying number

Part I Election To Expense Certain Property Under Section 179
Note: If you have any listed property, complete Part V before you complete Part I.

1	Maximum amount (see instructions)	1
2	Total cost of section 179 property placed in service (see instructions)	2
3	Threshold cost of section 179 property before reduction in limitation (see instructions)	3
4	Reduction in limitation. Subtract line 3 from line 2. If zero or less, enter -0-	4
5	Dollar limitation for tax year. Subtract line 4 from line 1. If zero or less, enter -0-. If married filing separately, see instructions	5

6	(a) Description of property	(b) Cost (business use only)	(c) Elected cost

7	Listed property. Enter the amount from line 29	7	
8	Total elected cost of section 179 property. Add amounts in column (c), lines 6 and 7	8
9	Tentative deduction. Enter the **smaller** of line 5 or line 8	9
10	Carryover of disallowed deduction from line 13 of your 2022 Form 4562	10
11	Business income limitation. Enter the smaller of business income (not less than zero) or line 5. See instructions	11
12	Section 179 expense deduction. Add lines 9 and 10, but don't enter more than line 11	12
13	Carryover of disallowed deduction to 2024. Add lines 9 and 10, less line 12 .	13	

Note: Don't use Part II or Part III below for listed property. Instead, use Part V.

Part II Special Depreciation Allowance and Other Depreciation (Don't include listed property. See instructions.)

14	Special depreciation allowance for qualified property (other than listed property) placed in service during the tax year. See instructions . . .	14
15	Property subject to section 168(f)(1) election	15
16	Other depreciation (including ACRS)	16

Part III MACRS Depreciation (Don't include listed property. See instructions.)

Section A

17	MACRS deductions for assets placed in service in tax years beginning before 2023	17
18	If you are electing to group any assets placed in service during the tax year into one or more general asset accounts, check here . . . . ☐	

Section B—Assets Placed in Service During 2023 Tax Year Using the General Depreciation System

(a) Classification of property	(b) Month and year placed in service	(c) Basis for depreciation (business/investment use only—see instructions)	(d) Recovery period	(e) Convention	(f) Method	(g) Depreciation deduction
19a 3-year property						
b 5-year property						
c 7-year property						
d 10-year property						
e 15-year property						
f 20-year property						
g 25-year property			25 yrs.		S/L	
h Residential rental property			27.5 yrs.	MM	S/L	
			27.5 yrs.	MM	S/L	
i Nonresidential real property			39 yrs.	MM	S/L	
				MM	S/L	

Section C—Assets Placed in Service During 2023 Tax Year Using the Alternative Depreciation System

20a Class life					S/L	
b 12-year			12 yrs.		S/L	
c 30-year			30 yrs.	MM	S/L	
d 40-year			40 yrs.	MM	S/L	

Part IV Summary (See instructions.)

21	Listed property. Enter amount from line 28	21
22	**Total.** Add amounts from line 12, lines 14 through 17, lines 19 and 20 in column (g), and line 21. Enter here and on the appropriate lines of your return. Partnerships and S corporations—see instructions	22
23	For assets shown above and placed in service during the current year, enter the portion of the basis attributable to section 263A costs	23	

For Paperwork Reduction Act Notice, see separate instructions.   Cat. No. 12906N   Form **4562** (2023)

Part V Listed Property (Include automobiles, certain other vehicles, certain aircraft, and property used for entertainment, recreation, or amusement.)

Note: For any vehicle for which you are using the standard mileage rate or deducting lease expense, complete **only** 24a, 24b, columns (a) through (c) of Section A, all of Section B, and Section C if applicable.

Section A—Depreciation and Other Information (Caution: See the instructions for limits for passenger automobiles.)

24a Do you have evidence to support the business/investment use claimed? ☐ Yes ☐ No						24b If "Yes," is the evidence written? ☐ Yes ☐ No		
(a) Type of property (list vehicles first)	(b) Date placed in service	(c) Business/ investment use percentage	(d) Cost or other basis	(e) Basis for depreciation (business/investment use only)	(f) Recovery period	(g) Method/ Convention	(h) Depreciation deduction	(i) Elected section 179 cost
25 Special depreciation allowance for qualified listed property placed in service during the tax year and used more than 50% in a qualified business use. See instructions .					25			
26 Property used more than 50% in a qualified business use:								
		%						
		%						
		%						
27 Property used 50% or less in a qualified business use:								
		%				S/L –		
		%				S/L –		
		%				S/L –		
28 Add amounts in column (h), lines 25 through 27. Enter here and on line 21, page 1 .					28			
29 Add amounts in column (i), line 26. Enter here and on line 7, page 1 .							29	

Section B—Information on Use of Vehicles

Complete this section for vehicles used by a sole proprietor, partner, or other "more than 5% owner," or related person. If you provided vehicles to your employees, first answer the questions in Section C to see if you meet an exception to completing this section for those vehicles.

	(a) Vehicle 1		(b) Vehicle 2		(c) Vehicle 3		(d) Vehicle 4		(e) Vehicle 5		(f) Vehicle 6	
30 Total business/investment miles driven during the year (**don't** include commuting miles) .												
31 Total commuting miles driven during the year												
32 Total other personal (noncommuting) miles driven												
33 Total miles driven during the year. Add lines 30 through 32												
34 Was the vehicle available for personal use during off-duty hours?	Yes	No	Yes	No	Yes	No	Yes	No	Yes	No	Yes	No
35 Was the vehicle used primarily by a more than 5% owner or related person? . .												
36 Is another vehicle available for personal use?												

Section C—Questions for Employers Who Provide Vehicles for Use by Their Employees

Answer these questions to determine if you meet an exception to completing Section B for vehicles used by employees who **aren't** more than 5% owners or related persons. See instructions.

		Yes	No
37 Do you maintain a written policy statement that prohibits all personal use of vehicles, including commuting, by your employees?			
38 Do you maintain a written policy statement that prohibits personal use of vehicles, except commuting, by your employees? See the instructions for vehicles used by corporate officers, directors, or 1% or more owners . .			
39 Do you treat all use of vehicles by employees as personal use?			
40 Do you provide more than five vehicles to your employees, obtain information from your employees about the use of the vehicles, and retain the information received?			
41 Do you meet the requirements concerning qualified automobile demonstration use? See instructions			

Note: If your answer to 37, 38, 39, 40, or 41 is "Yes," don't complete Section B for the covered vehicles.

Part VI Amortization

(a) Description of costs	(b) Date amortization begins	(c) Amortizable amount	(d) Code section	(e) Amortization period or percentage	(f) Amortization for this year
42 Amortization of costs that begins during your 2023 tax year (see instructions):					
43 Amortization of costs that began before your 2023 tax year				43	
44 **Total.** Add amounts in column (f). See the instructions for where to report				44	

Form **4562** (2023)

46

Chapter 7: Understanding the Passive Activity Loss Rules for Rental Properties

Passive vs. Active Participation: IRS Definitions and Rules

When it comes to renting out living space on platforms like Airbnb, understanding the difference between passive and active participation is crucial for tax purposes. The Internal Revenue Service (IRS) has specific definitions and rules in place that determine how your rental income is treated and what deductions you can take. Let's delve into the details to ensure you stay on the right side of the taxman.

Passive participation refers to situations where you are not materially involved in the day-to-day operations of your rental property. This could apply if you hire a property management company to handle bookings, guest communication, and maintenance. In this case, the income generated from your rental would be considered passive income. It is important to note that passive rental income may be subject to the Net Investment Income Tax (NIIT) if your modified adjusted gross income exceeds certain thresholds.

On the other hand, active participation occurs when you are significantly involved in managing your rental property. This includes tasks such as screening guests, advertising the listing, and performing regular maintenance. If you actively participate in your Airbnb rental, the income is treated differently. It is considered nonpassive income, which means it is not subject to the NIIT. This distinction can have significant tax implications, especially if your rental income is your primary source of income.

Understanding the IRS definitions is crucial for maximizing your tax deductions. As an STR host, you are eligible for various deductions, such as property expenses, maintenance costs, and even a portion of your home office if you use it exclusively for your rental activities. However, the specific deductions available to you depend on whether your rental income is considered passive or active.

Additionally, tax rules can vary from country to country or state to state. If you operate in multiple locations, it is important to familiarize yourself with the tax considerations and reporting requirements specific to each jurisdiction. This will help you avoid any potential penalties or compliance issues.

In conclusion, knowing the difference between passive and active participation is essential for STR hosts. By understanding the IRS definitions and rules, you can accurately report your rental income and maximize your tax deductions. Remember to consult with a tax professional who specializes in short-term rentals to ensure you stay compliant with the ever-changing tax landscape.

Limitations and Exceptions to the Passive Activity Loss Rules

As an STR host, it is essential to understand the limitations and exceptions to the passive activity loss rules when it comes to your tax obligations. The passive activity loss rules were established by the Internal Revenue Service (IRS) to determine how rental income and expenses are treated for tax purposes. These rules are important to ensure that you stay compliant and maximize your tax deductions as an STR host. Here are some key points to consider:

1. Material Participation: To be able to deduct rental losses against your active income, you must meet the material participation test. This test requires you to participate in the rental activity on a regular, continuous, and substantial basis. Meeting this test allows you to offset your rental losses against your other income.

2. Active Participation: If you do not meet the material participation test, you may still be able to deduct up to $25,000 of rental losses if you actively participate in the rental activity. Active participation includes making management decisions, such as approving new guests, setting rental rates, and arranging repairs.

3. Phase-Out Limitations: The $25,000 deduction for active participants starts to phase out once your modified adjusted gross income (MAGI) exceeds $100,000 and is completely phased out at $150,000. It is important to carefully track your MAGI to determine if you qualify for this deduction.

4. Real Estate Professionals: If you qualify as a real estate professional, you are not subject to the passive activity loss rules. To meet this qualification, you must spend more than 750 hours per year in real estate activities and more than half of your working time in real estate trades or businesses.

5. Vacation Homes and Second Properties: If you rent out a vacation home or a second property on Airbnb, special rules may apply. The number of days you personally use the property versus the number of days it is rented can impact the tax treatment. It is important to consult

with a tax professional to understand the specific rules that apply to your situation.

Understanding the limitations and exceptions to the passive activity loss rules is crucial for STR hosts. By familiarizing yourself with these rules, you can maximize your tax deductions, ensure compliance, and potentially reduce your tax liability. Remember to keep detailed records of your rental activity, expenses, and income to support your tax reporting and filing. Consult with a tax professional who specializes in STR hosts and rental properties to navigate the complexities of tax implications in different countries or states and to develop effective tax strategies.

Strategies for Utilizing Passive Activity Losses

As an STR host, understanding the tax implications and finding ways to maximize deductions is crucial to save money and stay compliant with the tax laws. One strategy that can greatly benefit hosts is utilizing passive activity losses. This subchapter will explore various strategies to help STR hosts make the most of passive activity losses and reduce their taxable income.

Passive activity losses occur when the expenses incurred in generating rental income exceed the rental income itself. These losses can often be deducted against other passive income, such as rental income from other properties or investments. Here are some strategies for utilizing passive activity losses:

1. Rental property grouping: If you have multiple rental properties, consider grouping them together as a single activity. This allows you to

offset the losses from one property against the income generated by another, potentially reducing your overall taxable income.

2. Real estate professional status: If you meet certain criteria and spend a significant amount of time on real estate activities, you may qualify as a real estate professional. This status allows you to deduct all your rental losses against any type of income, not just passive income.

3. Active participation: If you actively participate in the management of your rental activity, you may be able to deduct up to $25,000 in rental losses against your non-passive income, such as wages or business income.

4. Material participation: If you meet the criteria for material participation, you can deduct all rental losses against any type of income. This requires substantial involvement in the rental activity, such as spending more than 500 hours per year on rental-related tasks.

5. Carryforward losses: If you have passive activity losses that cannot be fully utilized in the current year, you can carry them forward to future years. This allows you to offset future rental income or gains from property sales.

Remember, tax laws can vary between countries and states, so it's essential to consult with a tax professional familiar with STR hosting and local tax regulations. They can help you navigate the complex tax landscape and develop a personalized tax strategy to maximize deductions.

By utilizing passive activity losses effectively, STR hosts can significantly reduce their taxable income and save money on taxes. However, it's important to stay informed about tax regulations and seek professional advice to ensure compliance with the ever-changing tax laws in your jurisdiction.

Understanding Rental Property Losses and Their Tax Treatment

As a person who rents out living space to others, it is crucial to have a clear understanding of rental property losses and how they are treated for tax purposes. This subchapter aims to provide you with valuable insights into this topic, ensuring that you can maximize your tax deductions and stay compliant with the tax regulations.

One of the key aspects to comprehend is the tax treatment of rental property losses. Rental property losses occur when the expenses of renting out your property exceed the income generated from it. These losses can arise from various factors such as mortgage interest, property taxes, repairs, maintenance, and depreciation. Understanding how these losses are treated allows you to offset them against your other income, reducing your overall tax liability.

Strategizing Tax Benefits Hosts is an essential resource for individuals hosting on Airbnb, as it provides detailed guidance on tax deductions specifically tailored to STR hosts. It explores the various expenses that can be deducted, including cleaning fees, advertising costs, insurance premiums, and even home office expenses if you use a portion of your home exclusively for your Airbnb business.

In addition to tax deductions, the book also covers tax reporting and filing requirements for Airbnb income. It helps you navigate the complex world of tax reporting, ensuring that you accurately report your rental income and comply with the tax regulations. Furthermore, it addresses the tax implications of renting out a room in your primary residence on Airbnb, delving into the specific rules and regulations that apply in such cases.

The book also offers valuable insights into tax considerations for Airbnb hosts in different countries or states. Tax laws can vary significantly depending on your location, and being aware of the specific tax regulations in your area is crucial. Whether you are an Airbnb host in the United States, Europe, or any other part of the world, this subchapter provides you with the necessary information to understand your tax obligations and make informed decisions.

Furthermore, Strategizing Tax Benefits explores tax strategies for maximizing deductions, such as keeping detailed records of your expenses, utilizing depreciation, and taking advantage of available tax credits. It also highlights tax benefits and incentives for eco-friendly Airbnb hosts, recognizing the importance of sustainable practices and offering potential tax advantages for those who incorporate them into their hosting activities.

For STR hosts who also rent out their property on other platforms, the book provides comprehensive tax planning strategies to ensure that you effectively manage your tax obligations while optimizing your deductions. It covers the tax implications of renting out a vacation home or second property on Airbnb or Vrbo, addressing the unique considerations and potential tax advantages associated with these scenarios.

Additionally, if you host events or parties on your property, the book offers essential tax tips to help you navigate the tax implications of such activities. It explains how to properly account for income generated from events and parties and provides guidance on deductible expenses related to hosting these gatherings.

Finally, for those who rent out a portion of their property or a shared space on Airbnb, the book explores the specific tax implications and deductions available in such situations. It provides clarity on how to allocate expenses and report income accurately, ensuring that you comply with the tax regulations while maximizing your deductions.

This subchapter, provides invaluable guidance for people who rent out living space to others. Whether you are an Airbnb host or using other platforms, this chapter of Tax Tips for Airbnb Hosts equips you with the knowledge and strategies necessary to effectively manage your tax obligations, maximize deductions, and stay compliant with the tax regulations.

Passive Activity Loss Limitations and Carryover Rules

As an Airbnb host, it's important to understand the passive activity loss limitations and carryover rules that may affect your tax situation. These rules can impact the amount of deductions you can claim and how you can carry forward any losses you incur.

Passive activity refers to any activity in which you do not materially participate. This includes renting out living spaces on Airbnb, as it typically does not require your constant involvement. The Internal Revenue Service (IRS) has established specific rules regarding passive activity losses to prevent taxpayers from using rental losses to offset other types of income.

Under the passive activity loss limitations, you can only deduct losses from your rental activities up to the amount of income you generate from those activities. In other words, if your rental income exceeds your rental expenses, you can deduct the full amount of those expenses.

However, if your rental expenses exceed your rental income, the excess loss may be limited.

The IRS categorizes rental activities into two groups: passive and non-passive. If you actively participate in the rental activity, you may be able to deduct up to $25,000 of rental losses against your non-passive income, such as wages or business income. However, this deduction is subject to a phase-out threshold based on your modified adjusted gross income (MAGI). If your MAGI exceeds the threshold, the deduction is gradually reduced until it is completely phased out.

If you do not meet the criteria for active participation or your MAGI exceeds the threshold, your rental losses are considered passive losses. These losses can only be used to offset passive income, such as income from other rental properties or limited partnerships. Any excess passive losses that you cannot currently deduct can be carried forward and used to offset future passive income.

It's important to keep accurate records of your rental activities, including income and expenses, to properly calculate your passive activity losses. Additionally, consult with a tax professional to ensure you understand the specific rules and limitations that apply to your situation.

In conclusion, understanding the passive activity loss limitations and carryover rules is crucial for Airbnb hosts. By familiarizing yourself with these rules, you can maximize your deductions and ensure compliance with the tax regulations applicable to your rental activities.

Strategies for Offset and Utilization of Rental Property Losses

One of the key aspects of being a successful Airbnb host is understanding the tax implications and maximizing deductions to save money and stay compliant. As a host who rents out living space to others, it is important to be aware of strategies for offsetting and utilizing rental property losses to your advantage. In this subchapter, we will explore some effective strategies that can help you minimize your tax liability and make the most of your rental property losses.

When it comes to tax deductions for Airbnb hosts, it is essential to keep careful track of all expenses related to your rental property. This includes maintenance and repair costs, utilities, insurance, property management fees, and even depreciation. By accurately documenting these expenses, you can offset your rental income and potentially generate a loss.

One strategy to utilize rental property losses is to carry them forward to future years. If your rental property generates a loss in a particular tax year, you may be able to carry that loss forward and deduct it against future rental income. This can help reduce your taxable income and potentially result in significant tax savings over time.

Another strategy is to actively participate in the management of your rental property. By meeting certain criteria set by the IRS, you can qualify as a real estate professional and potentially deduct rental losses against your other sources of income, such as your day job. This can be particularly beneficial for hosts who have a regular job and rely on their rental income as a secondary source of income.

Additionally, it is important to explore any tax benefits and incentives available for eco-friendly STR hosts. Many jurisdictions offer tax credits or deductions for hosts who make environmentally friendly upgrades to their rental properties, such as installing energy-efficient appliances or solar panels. Taking advantage of these incentives can not only help you save money on taxes but also attract eco-conscious guests.

Lastly, if you rent out a vacation home or a second property on Airbnb, there may be unique tax implications to consider. It is crucial to understand the rules and regulations specific to your location and consult with a tax professional to ensure compliance and maximize deductions.

In conclusion, as an STR host, understanding strategies for offsetting and utilizing rental property losses can have a significant impact on your tax liability. By carefully tracking expenses, carrying forward losses, qualifying as a real estate professional, exploring eco-friendly incentives, and being aware of vacation home tax implications, you can effectively minimize your tax liability and maximize your deductions as an STR host. Remember, it is always advisable to consult with a tax professional who specializes in STR taxation to ensure you are taking full advantage of all available strategies and staying compliant with the tax laws in your jurisdiction.

Chapter 8: IRS Rules on Rental Property Depreciation Recapture

Depreciation Recapture: Definition and Calculation

As an STR host, it's crucial to understand the concept of depreciation recapture and its implications for your tax obligations. Depreciation recapture refers to the process of reclaiming the tax benefits you previously enjoyed from depreciating your rental property or a portion of it. This subchapter will provide you with a comprehensive understanding of depreciation recapture, its definition, and how to calculate it accurately.

Definition of Depreciation Recapture:
Depreciation is an accounting method used to spread the cost of an asset over its useful life. When you own a rental property, you can deduct a portion of its value each year as depreciation on your tax return. However, if you sell the property or stop renting it out, you must recapture the depreciation deductions you previously claimed.

Calculation of Depreciation Recapture:
The calculation of depreciation recapture depends on various factors, including the depreciation method used, the period of ownership, and the sale price of the property. Generally, the recapture amount is determined by comparing the property's adjusted basis (original purchase price minus depreciation deductions) with the sale price.

To calculate depreciation recapture, follow these steps:

1. Determine the adjusted basis of your property: Start with the original purchase price and subtract the total depreciation deductions claimed over the years.

2. Determine the property's fair market value at the time of sale: This is the sale price or the amount you received from the sale.

3. Compare the adjusted basis with the fair market value: If the fair market value is higher than the adjusted basis, you have a potential gain subject to depreciation recapture.

4. Calculate the recapture amount: Multiply the potential gain by the depreciation recapture tax rate. The recapture tax rate is typically 25% for real estate properties.

It's important to note that depreciation recapture is considered ordinary income, subject to your regular income tax rate. Therefore, it's crucial to consult with a tax professional or use tax software to accurately calculate and report depreciation recapture on your tax return.

Understanding depreciation recapture is essential for STR hosts, as it can significantly impact your tax liabilities. By staying informed about depreciation recapture and consulting with tax experts, you can stay compliant with tax regulations and minimize any potential surprises during tax season.

Remember, tax laws and regulations can vary between countries and states. Be sure to research and understand the specific tax considerations and implications for STR hosts in your jurisdiction to maximize your deductions and comply with the applicable tax laws.

Identifying Triggers for Depreciation Recapture

As an STR host, you are likely aware of the various tax implications and responsibilities that come with renting out your living space. One important aspect to consider is depreciation recapture, which refers to the potential tax consequences when you sell or dispose of a property that you have been depreciating.

Depreciation recapture occurs when you have claimed depreciation deductions on your rental property and then sell it for a gain. The IRS requires you to recapture a portion of the depreciation deductions you have taken over the years as ordinary income. This means you may be subject to higher tax rates on this recaptured amount.

To better understand how depreciation recapture may affect you as an STR host, it is crucial to identify the triggers that can lead to this tax consequence. Here are a few scenarios that may result in depreciation recapture:

1. Selling your rental property: If you decide to sell your property, any gain from the sale will trigger depreciation recapture. This includes not only the actual sale of your property but also if you transfer it to someone else, convert it to personal use, or abandon it.

2. Converting your rental property to personal use: If you decide to stop renting out your property and use it as your primary residence or vacation home, depreciation recapture may come into play. The IRS treats this conversion as a disposition of the property, potentially triggering recapture.

3. Exchanging your rental property: If you participate in a like-kind exchange, also known as a 1031 exchange, where you replace your rental property with another investment property, you may still be subject to depreciation recapture. This is because the IRS requires you to account for the depreciation taken on the original property.

4. Transferring ownership of your rental property: If you transfer the ownership of your rental property to a corporation, partnership, or another entity, depreciation recapture may apply. The IRS considers this transfer as a disposition, potentially triggering recapture.

Understanding these triggers for depreciation recapture is essential for proper tax planning as an STR host. By being aware of the potential consequences, you can make informed decisions about your rental property and take advantage of the available tax strategies to minimize your tax liability.

Please note that tax laws and regulations vary by country and state, so it is advisable to consult with a tax professional who specializes in STR taxation to ensure compliance and maximize your deductions. Being proactive in your tax planning can help you stay compliant while saving money as an STR host.

Strategies for Managing and Minimizing Depreciation Recapture Taxes

One important aspect of being an STR host is understanding the tax implications of renting out your property. Depreciation recapture taxes can be a significant consideration for hosts, so it is crucial to have strategies in place to manage and minimize these taxes. This subchapter will provide valuable insights and tips for hosts to navigate this complex area of taxation.

1. Understanding Depreciation Recapture Taxes: Depreciation is the gradual loss of value in a property over time. When you rent out your property, you can claim depreciation as an expense against your rental income. However, when you sell the property, you may be subject to depreciation recapture taxes, which means the IRS will recapture a portion of the depreciation deductions you previously claimed.

2. Utilizing a 1031 Exchange: A 1031 exchange allows you to defer depreciation recapture taxes by reinvesting the proceeds from the sale of your property into a like-kind property. This strategy can be particularly beneficial for hosts who wish to upgrade or diversify their rental property portfolio.

3. Proper Record-Keeping: Accurate record-keeping is essential to support your depreciation deductions and ensure you are correctly reporting your rental income. Maintain detailed records of your property's purchase price, improvements, rental income, and any expenses related to the property.

4. Claiming Qualified Business Income Deduction: The Tax Cuts and Jobs Act introduced the Qualified Business Income (QBI) deduction, which allows eligible hosts to deduct up to 20% of their rental income. Understanding the criteria for claiming this deduction can help reduce your overall tax liability.

5. Consult with a Tax Professional: The tax landscape can be complex, especially for STR hosts. Seeking advice from a tax professional who specializes in rental income and real estate taxation can provide valuable guidance tailored to your specific circumstances. They can help you navigate depreciation recapture taxes and identify additional strategies to minimize your tax burden.

By implementing these strategies, STR hosts can effectively manage and minimize depreciation recapture taxes. Being proactive and staying informed about the latest tax regulations and incentives can help hosts optimize their tax planning, maximize deductions, and stay compliant with the tax authorities. Remember, this subchapter serves as a general guide, and it is always prudent to consult with a tax professional for personalized advice based on your unique situation.

Chapter 9: Tax Planning for STR Hosts Renting Out Property on Other Platforms

Tax Implications of Renting Out Property on Multiple Platforms

Renting out living space to other people has become increasingly popular with the rise of platforms such as Airbnb. However, as a host, it is important to understand the tax implications of renting out your property on multiple platforms. This subchapter will provide valuable insights and tax tips for individuals who rent out living spaces to others.

One of the key considerations for STR hosts is tax deductions. By renting out your property, you may be eligible for various deductions that can help you save money. This subchapter will explore the different tax deductions available for STR hosts and provide strategies for maximizing these deductions. From home office expenses to repairs and maintenance, knowing which deductions to claim can result in significant tax savings.

Additionally, tax reporting and filing for STR income is another crucial aspect. As an STR host, you are required to report your rental income to the tax authorities. This subchapter will guide you through the process of reporting and filing your STR income correctly, ensuring compliance with tax regulations. It will also address any specific requirements for reporting STR income in different countries or states, providing a comprehensive understanding of the tax reporting process.

Moreover, this subchapter will delve into the tax implications of renting out a room in your primary residence on Airbnb. Renting out a portion of your property or a shared space may have different tax considerations compared to renting out the entire property. Understanding these implications is essential for proper tax planning and compliance.

Furthermore, for those hosts who rent out their property on multiple platforms, this subchapter will provide tax planning strategies. It will explore the tax implications of renting out a vacation home or second property on platforms like Airbnb, as well as other platforms. By implementing proper tax planning strategies, you can minimize your tax liability while maximizing your rental income.

Lastly, this subchapter will address specific tax tips for STR hosts who host events or parties on their property. Renting out your property for events may have unique tax implications that are important to understand to stay compliant with tax regulations.

In summary, this book provides valuable insights into the tax implications of renting out property on multiple platforms. Whether you are renting out a room in your primary residence, a vacation home, or hosting events on your property, understanding the tax implications is crucial for saving money and staying compliant with tax regulations. By following the tax tips and strategies provided in this subchapter, you can navigate the complexities of rental income taxation and maximize your deductions as an STR host.

Strategies for Managing Taxes when Using Multiple Rental Platforms

When you rent out living space to other people on multiple rental platforms, it's important to have a solid understanding of the tax implications and develop strategies to manage your taxes effectively. By following these strategies, you can save money and stay compliant with the tax laws in your country or state.

1. Keep Detailed Records: Maintaining accurate records is crucial for managing your taxes when renting out living space. Keep track of all rental income, expenses, and any other relevant financial transactions. This will help you determine the correct amount of taxable income and ensure you claim all eligible deductions.

2. Understand Tax Deductions: Familiarize yourself with the tax deductions available for Airbnb hosts or those renting out living space. These deductions can include expenses related to cleaning, repairs, maintenance, insurance, utilities, and even professional services like legal or accounting fees. By maximizing your deductions, you can reduce your overall tax liability.

3. Separate Personal and Rental Expenses: If you're renting out a portion of your primary residence or a shared space, it's essential to keep your personal and rental expenses separate. This will help you accurately determine the deductible portion of expenses and avoid any potential red flags during a tax audit.

4. Research Tax Laws in Different Countries or States: If you operate rentals in different countries or states, be aware that tax laws may vary. Take the time to research and understand the tax regulations specific to

each location. This knowledge will enable you to comply with the tax rules and take advantage of any available tax benefits or incentives.

5. Plan for Vacation Homes or Second Properties: Renting out a vacation home or second property on Airbnb can have different tax implications. Consult with a tax professional to ensure you understand the specific tax rules and determine the most advantageous tax strategies for managing these types of rentals.

6. Stay Updated on Tax Reporting and Filing: Tax laws and regulations change frequently, so it's important to stay informed about any updates related to reporting and filing requirements for rental income. Consider consulting with a tax professional or using tax software specifically designed for Airbnb hosts to ensure accurate reporting and timely filing.

By implementing these strategies for managing taxes when using multiple rental platforms, you can optimize your tax situation as a host and ensure compliance with the tax laws applicable to your rental activities. Remember, seeking advice from a qualified tax professional is always beneficial to ensure you make informed decisions and minimize your tax liability.

Reporting and Deducting Income from Other Rental Platforms

When it comes to renting out living space to other people, there are several important tax considerations to keep in mind. While the focus of this book is on STR hosting, it's worth noting that many hosts also utilize other rental platforms to maximize their rental income. In this subchapter, we will explore the reporting and deducting income from these other rental platforms.

First and foremost, it's crucial to understand that any income you earn from renting out your property, whether it's through Airbnb or another platform, is considered taxable. This means you are required to report this income to the tax authorities. Failure to report your rental income can result in penalties and interest charges, so it's essential to stay compliant.

When it comes to reporting your income, the process may vary depending on the platform you use. Some platforms, like Airbnb, provide hosts with a detailed transaction history and even issue 1099 forms for tax reporting purposes. However, other platforms may not offer these services, requiring hosts to keep meticulous records of their income and expenses.

Once you have accurately reported your rental income, it's time to consider the deductions you may be eligible for. As a rental property owner, you can deduct various expenses related to your rental activity, such as property taxes, mortgage interest, insurance premiums, repairs, and maintenance costs. These deductions can significantly reduce your taxable income and help you save money on your tax bill.

It's important to note that deductions may vary depending on whether you rent out a room in your primary residence, a vacation home, or a second property. Additionally, the tax implications of renting out a portion of your property or a shared space can differ from renting out the entire property.

Furthermore, if you host events or parties on your property, there may be additional tax considerations to keep in mind. Depending on the nature of these events, you may need to report the income separately and comply with specific regulations.

Lastly, it's worth mentioning that tax laws and regulations can vary from country to country and even from state to state. If you operate in multiple locations, it is essential to familiarize yourself with the specific tax rules and requirements of each jurisdiction.

In conclusion, renting out living space on various rental platforms can be financially rewarding. However, it also comes with tax obligations that must be met. By accurately reporting your income and maximizing your deductions, you can save money and stay compliant with the tax authorities. Remember to consult with a tax professional to ensure you are taking advantage of all the tax strategies and incentives available to you as an Airbnb host.

Chapter 10: Tax Implications of Renting Out a Vacation Home or Second Property

Understanding Tax Rules for Vacation Home Rentals

Renting out a vacation home or second property on Airbnb can be a great way to generate income and make the most of your investment. However, it is important to understand the tax rules and implications associated with this type of rental activity. In this subchapter, we will delve into the specific tax considerations for Airbnb hosts who rent out vacation homes or second properties.

One of the key aspects to be aware of is the distinction between personal use and rental use of your vacation home. If you use the property for personal purposes for more than the greater of 14 days or 10% of the total days rented to others at a fair rental price, you will need to allocate expenses between personal and rental use. This means that you can only deduct expenses that are directly related to the rental portion of your property, such as advertising fees, cleaning costs, and property management fees.

Additionally, if you rent out your vacation home for less than 15 days during the year, you are not required to report the rental income on your tax return. This can be beneficial for hosts who only rent out their property for a short period, such as during a popular event or holiday season.

However, if you rent out your vacation home for more than 14 days, you will need to report the rental income on your tax return. You will also be eligible to deduct certain expenses, such as mortgage interest, property taxes, insurance, and repairs, based on the percentage of time your property is rented out versus used for personal purposes.

It is crucial to keep accurate records of your rental income and expenses, as well as any supporting documentation, such as receipts and invoices. This will not only help you accurately report your rental income but also maximize your deductions and potentially avoid any discrepancies during an audit.

Furthermore, it is important to note that tax rules for vacation home rentals on Airbnb can vary depending on the country or state in which you reside. Therefore, it is essential to consult with a tax professional or accountant who is familiar with the specific tax laws and regulations in your jurisdiction.

In conclusion, understanding the tax rules for vacation home rentals on Airbnb is essential for STR hosts who rent out living space to other people. By familiarizing yourself with the tax deductions, reporting and filing requirements, and other tax implications associated with renting out a vacation home or second property, you can ensure that you stay compliant with the tax laws and maximize your tax benefits as an Airbnb host.

Deductions and Reporting Requirements for Vacation Home Rentals

Renting out a vacation home can be a great way to earn extra income while also enjoying the benefits of owning a second property. However, it's important to understand the deductions and reporting requirements involved to ensure you stay compliant with the tax laws. In this subchapter, we will explore the various tax tips and strategies specifically tailored for Airbnb hosts who rent out vacation homes.

One of the key aspects of maximizing your tax deductions as a vacation home host is to keep detailed records of all expenses related to your rental property. This includes expenses such as mortgage interest, property taxes, insurance, repairs, and maintenance. By tracking these expenses, you can deduct them from your rental income, reducing your overall tax liability.

Additionally, if you use your vacation home for personal use as well, you will need to determine the number of days you rent it out versus the number of days you use it personally. This will affect the amount of deductions you can claim. For example, if you rent out your vacation home for more than 14 days a year and use it personally for less than 14 days or 10% of the total days rented, you can deduct expenses up to the amount of rental income received.

When it comes to reporting your vacation home rental income, you will need to include it on your tax return. This can be done using Schedule E, which is specifically designed for reporting rental income and expenses. It's crucial to accurately report your rental income to avoid any potential audits or penalties.

It's also worth noting that tax rules and regulations for vacation home rentals can vary from country to country or even state to state. Therefore, it's essential to understand the specific tax considerations and requirements in your jurisdiction. Working with a tax professional who specializes in vacation home rentals can provide valuable guidance and ensure you stay compliant with local tax laws.

In conclusion, understanding the deductions and reporting requirements for vacation home rentals is essential for Airbnb hosts. By keeping detailed records of expenses, properly reporting rental income, and staying informed about tax regulations, you can maximize your deductions and minimize your tax liability. Stay tuned for the next chapters to explore additional tax tips and strategies for Airbnb hosts in different scenarios and niches.

Tax Considerations for Converting a Second Property into a Rental on Airbnb

If you are one of the many people who rent out living space to others on Airbnb, you may be considering converting a second property into a rental. This can be a great way to generate extra income, but it's important to understand the tax considerations that come along with it. In this subchapter, we will explore the various tax implications and strategies for Airbnb hosts who convert a second property into a rental.

First and foremost, it's crucial to keep accurate records of all income and expenses related to your rental property. This includes rental income, cleaning fees, and any other payments you receive through the Airbnb platform. By maintaining detailed records, you can ensure that you report your income accurately and take advantage of all eligible deductions.

Speaking of deductions, there are several tax deductions available to Airbnb hosts. These include expenses such as mortgage interest, property taxes, insurance, utilities, repairs, and maintenance. It's essential to understand the rules surrounding each deduction and keep supporting documentation for all expenses claimed. By maximizing your deductions, you can minimize your taxable income and ultimately save money on your tax bill.

Reporting and filing your Airbnb income correctly is crucial to staying compliant with tax laws. Depending on your country or state, you may be required to report your rental income on your personal tax return or file a separate business tax return. It's important to consult with a tax professional or research the specific regulations in your jurisdiction to ensure you meet all reporting obligations.

If you are renting out a room in your primary residence on Airbnb, there may be additional tax implications to consider. Some countries or states have specific rules regarding the tax treatment of this type of rental income. For example, you may be eligible for a portion of the home office deduction if you use a dedicated space in your home for your STR business. Understanding these nuances can help you make informed decisions and optimize your tax situation.

Lastly, if you are considering renting out a vacation home or second property on Airbnb, there may be unique tax considerations. These can include rules regarding the number of days the property is rented, personal use of the property, and depreciation deductions. It's essential to consult with a tax professional who specializes in rental properties to ensure you navigate these complexities correctly.

Converting a second property into a rental on Airbnb can be a lucrative endeavor, but it's important to understand the tax considerations involved. By keeping accurate records, maximizing deductions, and staying compliant with tax laws, you can ensure that your Airbnb business remains financially successful while minimizing your tax liability.

Chapter 11: Tax Benefits of Using a Property Management Company for Rental Properties

Evaluating the Advantages of Hiring a Property Management Company

As a person who rents out living space to other people, you may find yourself overwhelmed by the responsibilities that come with being an STR host. From managing bookings and dealing with guest inquiries to ensuring the property is well-maintained, the list of tasks can seem never-ending. This is where hiring a property management company can make a significant difference in your hosting experience.

One of the most significant advantages of hiring a property management company is the time and stress it can save you. These professionals specialize in managing rental properties and can take care of all the day-to-day tasks that come with hosting. They will handle guest communication, bookings, and inquiries, ensuring a smooth and efficient process. This allows you to focus on other aspects of your life or invest more time in growing your hosting business.

Furthermore, property management companies are well-versed in tax matters, making them an invaluable resource for STR hosts. They can provide expert advice on tax deductions specifically tailored to your hosting situation. Whether it's maximizing deductions for expenses related to your property, understanding tax reporting and filing requirements for Airbnb income, or navigating the tax implications of renting out a room in your primary residence, property management companies have the knowledge and expertise to ensure you stay compliant and save money on your taxes.

Another advantage of hiring a property management company is their ability to handle various tax considerations for STR hosts in different countries or states. Tax laws can vary significantly, and it can be challenging to keep up with the latest regulations. Property management companies are well-versed in local tax laws and can provide guidance on tax strategies to maximize your deductions based on your specific location.

Additionally, property management companies can assist you in understanding the tax implications of renting out a vacation home or second property on Airbnb. Owning multiple properties can introduce complex tax situations, and having a professional by your side can help you navigate these intricacies effectively.

Whether you're hosting events or parties on your property, renting out a portion of your property, or offering shared spaces on STR, a property management company can provide valuable advice on the tax implications associated with these scenarios. They can help you understand the tax tips specific to your situation and ensure you're taking full advantage of any available deductions.

In conclusion, hiring a property management company offers numerous advantages for STR hosts. From saving time and minimizing stress to providing expert tax advice and navigating complex tax considerations, these professionals can be a valuable asset to your hosting business. Consider evaluating your needs and exploring the benefits that a property management company can bring to your Airbnb hosting experience.

Deductibility of Property Management Fees and Expenses

As an Airbnb host, you understand the importance of maximizing your earnings while remaining compliant with tax regulations. One area where you can potentially save money is through the deductibility of property management fees and expenses. By understanding the tax implications and strategies associated with these deductions, you can make informed decisions that will benefit your bottom line.

Property management fees are an essential part of running a successful STR business. These fees are typically paid to third-party companies or individuals who handle various aspects of property management, such as advertising, guest communications, cleaning, and maintenance. The good news is that these fees are generally deductible as ordinary business expenses.

When it comes to deducting property management fees, it's important to keep detailed records and receipts. This will help support your claims in case of an audit. Additionally, it's crucial to differentiate between personal and business expenses. Only expenses directly related to your Airbnb rental are eligible for deductions.

In addition to property management fees, you may also be able to deduct other expenses associated with your STR business. These can include advertising costs, cleaning supplies, repairs, utilities, insurance, property taxes, and even home office expenses if you use a portion of your home exclusively for Airbnb purposes. Again, proper record-keeping is key to substantiating these deductions.

It's worth noting that tax regulations can vary between countries and states, so it's essential to stay informed about the specific rules and regulations that apply to your location. Consulting with a tax professional who specializes in STR tax matters can be extremely beneficial in navigating the complexities of these deductions and ensuring compliance.

As an eco-friendly host, you may also be eligible for additional tax benefits and incentives. Some jurisdictions offer tax credits or deductions for hosts who implement environmentally friendly practices, such as using energy-efficient appliances or utilizing renewable energy sources.

In conclusion, understanding the deductibility of property management fees and expenses is crucial for Airbnb hosts. By keeping meticulous records, understanding the tax regulations in your location, and seeking professional advice when needed, you can maximize your deductions and save money while staying compliant. Remember, every dollar saved in taxes is an extra dollar in your pocket.

Considerations for Hiring and Working with a Property Management Company

If you are a host who rents out living space to others, you may have considered hiring a property management company to handle the day-to-day operations of your STR business. This can be a wise decision, as it allows you to focus on providing a great guest experience while leaving the administrative and maintenance tasks to professionals. However, before you hire a property management company, there are several considerations you should keep in mind.

First and foremost, it is crucial to thoroughly research and vet any potential property management companies you are considering. Look for companies with experience in managing short-term rentals and a solid reputation within the industry. Read reviews, ask for references, and interview multiple companies to ensure you find one that aligns with your goals and values.

When working with a property management company, communication is key. Make sure to establish clear lines of communication from the beginning and determine how often you will receive updates on your property's performance. Additionally, discuss how the company handles guest inquiries and complaints, as their responsiveness can greatly impact your guests' experience.

Another important consideration is the fees and services offered by the property management company. While it is natural to focus on the cost, it is equally important to understand what services are included in that fee. Some companies may offer comprehensive services, including marketing, guest screening, cleaning, and maintenance, while others may only provide basic management. Consider your specific needs and budget when selecting a property management company.

Tax implications are also a crucial consideration when hiring a property management company. Ensure that the company has a clear understanding of the tax laws and regulations in your country or state. They should be able to provide guidance on tax reporting and filing for your Airbnb income, as well as any deductions or incentives you may be eligible for as a host.

Lastly, it is essential to establish a clear contract with the property management company. This should outline the responsibilities and expectations of both parties, including the duration of the agreement, termination clauses, and any additional fees or penalties. Review the contract carefully and seek legal advice if needed to ensure that your interests are protected.

In conclusion, hiring a property management company can be a valuable asset for Airbnb hosts. By thoroughly researching and vetting potential companies, establishing clear communication and expectations, understanding the fees and services offered, considering tax implications, and establishing a clear contract, hosts can confidently work with a property management company to save time, streamline operations, and maximize their rental income.

Chapter 12: Conclusion and Final Tips for Tax-Savvy STR Hosts

Recap of Key Tax Strategies and Considerations

As a host who rents out living space to other people, it is essential to have a good understanding of the various tax strategies and considerations to ensure you can maximize your deductions and stay compliant with the law. Here is a recap of some key tax tips for STR hosts:

1. Tax deductions: One of the most significant benefits of being an STR host is the ability to claim tax deductions. Keep track of all your expenses related to your hosting activities, including cleaning fees, maintenance costs, supplies, and even the portion of your utilities used for hosting. These deductions can significantly reduce your taxable income.

2. Reporting and filing: Make sure you report all your STR income accurately on your tax return. Airbnb provides hosts with a Form 1099-K, which details your earnings for the year. However, this form may not include all the necessary information, so it's crucial to keep thorough records of your income and expenses.

3. Tax implications of renting out a room in your primary residence: If you rent out a room in your primary residence on Airbnb, you may be eligible for certain tax benefits. For example, you can deduct a portion of your mortgage interest, property taxes, and home insurance. However, it's essential to be aware of any limitations or restrictions imposed by your local tax laws.

4. International and state tax considerations: If you are an STR host in different countries or states, be aware of the tax obligations specific to those regions. Each jurisdiction may have different rules regarding tax reporting, deductions, and liabilities. Consider consulting a tax professional who specializes in cross-border or state tax matters to ensure compliance.

5. Maximizing deductions: Explore all possible deductions available to you as an STR host. This could include expenses related to marketing your listing, professional fees, travel expenses, and even home office deductions if you use a portion of your property exclusively for your hosting activities.

6. Eco-friendly incentives: Some jurisdictions offer tax benefits and incentives for eco-friendly STR hosts. If you have made eco-friendly upgrades to your property, such as installing solar panels or energy-efficient appliances, you may be eligible for tax credits or deductions. Check with your local tax authority to see if you qualify.

Remember, tax planning and compliance are crucial for STR hosts. The tax implications can vary depending on the type of property, location, and various other factors. It is always recommended to consult with a qualified tax professional who can provide personalized advice based on your specific circumstances. By staying informed and implementing these tax strategies, you can save money and ensure a smooth tax filing process as an Airbnb host.

Final Tips for Homeowners to Optimize Tax Benefits

As a homeowner who rents out living space to other people, it is essential to understand the various tax benefits available to you. By maximizing deductions and staying compliant, you can save money and ensure a smooth tax reporting and filing process. Here are some final tips to help you optimize tax benefits as an Airbnb host.

1. Keep meticulous records: Maintain detailed records of your rental income, expenses, and any improvements you make to your property. This will make it easier to calculate your taxable income accurately and claim deductions.

2. Understand tax deductions: Familiarize yourself with the tax deductions available to Airbnb hosts. Common deductions include mortgage interest, property taxes, insurance premiums, cleaning fees, repairs, and maintenance expenses.

3. Separate personal and rental use: If you rent out a portion of your property or a shared space, such as a room or a guesthouse, ensure you can differentiate between personal and rental use. Only expenses related to the rental portion are eligible for deductions.

4. Know your local regulations: Different countries or states may have specific tax considerations for Airbnb hosts. Research and understand the specific tax rules and reporting requirements in your jurisdiction to avoid any penalties or non-compliance issues.

5. Explore eco-friendly tax benefits: If you adopt eco-friendly practices in your rental property, such as installing energy-efficient appliances or using renewable energy sources, you may qualify for additional tax benefits or incentives. Check with your local tax authorities to explore these options.

6. Consider tax planning for multiple rental platforms: If you list your property on multiple rental platforms besides Airbnb, consult a tax

professional to develop a tax planning strategy that maximizes deductions and minimizes tax liabilities across all platforms.

7. Be aware of event hosting tax implications: If you host events or parties on your property, be mindful of the tax implications. In certain cases, income generated from these events may be subject to different tax rates or additional reporting requirements.

8. Understand tax implications of renting out a vacation home: Renting out a vacation home or second property on Airbnb may have different tax considerations. Consult a tax expert to ensure you are aware of any specific rules or regulations that apply to your situation.

By following these final tips, you can optimize tax benefits and ensure compliance with tax regulations as a homeowner renting out living space. Remember to consult a tax professional for personalized advice based on your specific circumstances. With proper planning and documentation, you can make the most of your tax deductions and save money as an Airbnb host.

In conclusion, optimizing tax benefits for homeowners utilizing Airbnb and Vrbo requires careful planning and attention to detail. By understanding the rules surrounding reporting rental income, depreciation, deductible expenses, passive activity loss, and utilizing property management companies, you can ensure you're maximizing your tax benefits and minimizing your tax liability. Consult with a tax professional to tailor these tips to your specific situation and reap the full potential of tax benefits for your short-term rental income.

www.ingramcontent.com/pod-product-compliance
Lightning Source LLC
Chambersburg PA
CBHW062357290526
45794CB00005B/2259